ESSENTIAL LIBRARY OF THE
INFORMATION AGE

BIG DATA AND PRIVACY RIGHTS

by M. M. Eboch

CONTENT CONSULTANT
Dr. Scott J. Shackelford
Assistant Professor of
Business Law and Ethics
Kelley School of Business
Indiana University

Essential Library

An Imprint of Abdo Publishing | abdopublishing.com

abdopublishing.com

Published by Abdo Publishing, a division of ABDO, PO Box 398166, Minneapolis, Minnesota 55439. Copyright © 2017 by Abdo Consulting Group, Inc. International copyrights reserved in all countries. No part of this book may be reproduced in any form without written permission from the publisher. Essential Library™ is a trademark and logo of Abdo Publishing.

Printed in the United States of America, North Mankato, Minnesota
042016
092016

Cover Photo: Red Line Editorial
Interior Photos: Wolfgang Kumm/AP Images, 5; WikiLeaks/AP Images, 7; Bill Clark/CQ Roll Call/AP Images, 8; Pablo Martinez Monsivais/AP Images, 11; F. A. Brockhaus, 15; US Army, 17; Jason Doly/iStockphoto, 20; Julie Clopper/Shutterstock Images, 23; iStockphoto, 25, 31, 45, 71, 74, 81, 95, 99; Monkey Business Images/Shutterstock Images, 27; Suzy Oliveira/iStockphoto, 29; Shutterstock Images, 33; Olivier Douliery/Sipa USA/AP Images, 35; Jason Miller/National Council on Aging and Sanofi Pasteur/AP Images, 41; Altaf Qadri/AP Images, 43; Frank Franklin II/AP Images, 48; Yomiuri Shimbun/AP Images, 51; Charles Dharapak/AP Images, 53; PA Wire URN:11575499/AP Images, 55; Peter Haley/The News Tribune/AP Images, 57; M. Spencer Green/AP Images, 61; Gabe Hernandez/The Monitor/AP Images, 63; Jordan Strauss/Invision/AP Images, 65, 89; Giles Keyte/© Columbia Pictures Entertainment/Everett Collection, 67; Anna Bryukhanova/iStockphoto, 69; Chris Steer/iStockphoto, 79; Adam Gregor/Shutterstock Images, 85; David Ahn/iStockphoto, 87; J. Scott Applewhite/AP Images, 91; Thos Robinson/The Louise Blouin Foundation/Getty Images, 97

Editor: Elizabeth Dingmann Schneider
Series Designer: Craig Hinton

Publisher's Cataloging in Publication Data

Names: Eboch, M. M., author.
Title: Big data and privacy rights / by M. M. Eboch.
Description: Minneapolis, MN : Abdo Publishing, [2017] | Series: Essential library of the information age | Includes bibliographical references and index.
Identifiers: LCCN 2015960314 | ISBN 9781680782820 (lib. bdg.) | ISBN 9781680774719 (ebook)
Subjects: LCSH: Privacy, Right of--Juvenile literature. | Data protection--Juvenile literature.
Classification: DDC 323.44--dc23
LC record available at http://lccn.loc.gov/2015960314

CONTENTS

CHAPTER 1

SPIES ON THE INTERNET

Many Americans make phone calls, send texts and e-mails, and search the Internet on a daily basis. People tend to assume these activities are only of interest to the individuals directly involved. Or at least people thought this before June 2013.

That's when the news broke that the US National Security Agency (NSA) was spying on US citizens. The news was first reported in a British daily newspaper, the *Guardian*, and soon after in the *Washington Post*. The story describes extensive eavesdropping on communications. A secret court order had required the telecommunications company Verizon to give all of its telephone data to the NSA. The records were made available every day on an ongoing basis. Newspapers also reported the NSA had direct access to the servers at nine Internet firms.[1] A secret program called PRISM allowed the agency to collect information from companies such as Google, Microsoft, Apple, Yahoo, and Facebook. NSA officials could look at a user's search history and access the contents of e-mails, live chats, photos, videos, and file transfers.

A protester in Germany participates in a demonstration against NSA surveillance.

The President's Council of Advisors on Science and Technology noted several areas where privacy applies. One is the right to be left alone, which includes keeping personal matters and relationships secret. However, most people also want to be able to share information selectively. In other words, they want to choose who sees their personal information, rather than having it either completely private or else available to the general public. Another privacy right is the ability to express ideas and political opinions anonymously. There is also the right to make personal decisions without interference from the government or other organizations. Finally, privacy can involve protection from discrimination. This might involve keeping characteristics such as race or gender secret so the information cannot be used to discriminate. These are rights many scholars believe should exist. However, laws protect these rights to different degrees.

Later reports accused the United States of spying on European Union offices, 38 foreign targets (including many embassies), and 35 world leaders.[2] The NSA was also accused of hacking many government and private targets in Hong Kong and mainland China.

The man behind the revelations was Edward Snowden, a former Central Intelligence Agency (CIA) systems analyst, who provided government records to back his claims. The US government labeled him a traitor and charged him with crimes, including theft of government property. Some critics say his actions put the lives of American and British spies, and even ordinary citizens, at risk. Others hailed him as a hero for exposing America's questionable spying tactics. At the very least, by exposing the NSA's secret operations, Snowden set off a vigorous debate about the balance between security and privacy. Snowden, then 29 years old, went into hiding overseas. In October 2015,

Former NSA contractor Edward Snowden speaks in Russia in October 2013.

the European Parliament adopted a nonbinding resolution encouraging the European Union to protect Snowden from prosecution as a whistle-blower and a defender of human rights. However, the official US position remained unchanged.

MASSIVE DATA COLLECTION

The total amount of data collected was massive. In March 2013, the NSA collected 97 billion pieces of information from computer networks worldwide.[3] The main targets were Iran and Pakistan, but US allies were also included. An additional 3 billion pieces of data came from networks based in the United States.[4] Snowden said, "We hack everyone everywhere. We like to make a distinction

NSA surveillance protesters marched in Washington, DC, in October 2013.

between us and the others. But we are in almost every country in the world. We are not at war with these countries."[5]

The NSA had collected almost 200 million text messages each day from around the globe.[6] The NSA used these messages to gather information on the users' locations, contacts, and financial statuses. Much of the information collected came from people who were not under suspicion of any crimes. While US law gives the NSA legal authority

> ❝ I do not want to live in a world where everything I do and say is recorded. That is not something I am willing to support or live under. ❞ [7]
>
> —Edward Snowden

for some types of surveillance, the legal system is also intended to protect the privacy of innocent US citizens. However, the leaked documents suggested the NSA was breaking US privacy laws hundreds of times every year.[8] An internal NSA audit identified 2,776 violations of the rules or court orders regarding surveillance from April 2011 through March 2012.[9]

In the previous year, NSA representatives denied the NSA collected data on millions of Americans or even had the technical ability to intercept online communications in the United States. Yet according to Snowden, "The NSA has built an infrastructure that allows it to intercept almost everything. With this capability, the vast majority of human communications are automatically ingested without targeting. If I wanted to see your e-mails or your wife's phone, all I have to do is use intercepts.

PRIVACY PROTECTION

Privacy is protected by laws, including the Fourth Amendment to the US Constitution. This part of the Bill of Rights prohibits the US government from conducting unreasonable searches and seizures of property, including a person's home. The Fourth Amendment also requires search warrants to be based upon probable cause and to specifically describe what is to be searched or seized. The Internet age has introduced a new virtual home, which includes cloud storage. According to the President's Council of Advisors on Science and Technology, the Fourth Amendment protection of a person's home should logically extend to include property that is stored online. However, the Fourth Amendment has not yet been officially interpreted to protect the new virtual home.

FISA

The US government's powers of surveillance are detailed by laws, including the Foreign Intelligence Surveillance Act (FISA). FISA originally required the government to get a warrant before monitoring a US citizen's communications. The FISA Amendments Act, passed on July 10, 2008, greatly expanded the power of the NSA. The NSA could now access information directly without a warrant. In fact, it did not even have to ask the companies for access or let anyone know when it had accessed records.

Immediately after the 2008 amendments were enacted, the American Civil Liberties Union (ACLU) filed a lawsuit alleging the law was unconstitutional. The ACLU filed the case on behalf of a large group of human rights, legal, labor, and media organizations. In February 2013, the Supreme Court dismissed the ACLU's lawsuit.

The ACLU brought another lawsuit against the NSA after Edward Snowden revealed the extent of the NSA's spying on US citizens. A federal district court dismissed this lawsuit. In both cases, the courts stated the ACLU's clients did not have the standing to bring a lawsuit, because they could not show the NSA was monitoring their communications. As of 2016, the FISA Amendments Act stands, but the future may bring more challenges.

I can get your e-mails, passwords, phone records, credit cards."[10] From the telephone records, the government could see what calls were made but could not hear the conversations. Still, taken together, it meant the NSA could access nearly all of a person's communications. An official NSA statement denied any misuse of power, and many countries have similar surveillance programs.

PRIVACY VERSUS SECURITY

Some people feel the loss of privacy is worthwhile, especially when it comes to national security. Senator Dianne Feinstein wrote in a 2013 *Wall Street Journal* op-ed:

Senator Dianne Feinstein spoke out about the benefits of NSA surveillance with regard to national security.

Working in combination, the call-records database and other NSA programs have aided efforts by US intelligence agencies to disrupt terrorism in the US approximately a dozen times in recent years, according to the NSA. This summer, the agency disclosed that 54 terrorist events have been interrupted—including plots stopped and arrests made for support to terrorism.[11]

> "Criminals and terrorists would like nothing more than for us to miss out." [12]
> —James Comey, FBI director, criticizing technology that encrypts data

Despite those apparent successes, many people were

shaken by the idea that any agency could collect so much information on them. Most people do not participate in terrorism, spying, or other crimes. Innocent people wondered how much privacy they should have to give up in order to ensure a small number of criminals were caught.

Big data, or large sets of recorded information, is now everywhere. Data comes from e-mails, texts, phone calls, Internet search queries, social networking, and other online activity, such as watching videos or clicking on ads. Data may include location tracking through global positioning satellites in phones and computers. Data even comes from sensors in roads, bridges, homes, and clothing.

USA FREEDOM ACT

In June 2015, the USA Freedom Act was passed. It extended some sections of the Patriot Act, which allowed greater government surveillance in an attempt to prevent terrorism. However, the act stops the NSA from collecting massive amounts of phone data. Phone companies will retain the data, which the NSA can obtain only with permission from a federal court. Some critics say the new act does not do enough to control surveillance programs.

In nearly every aspect of life, from shopping to health care to social interactions, big data has provided both benefits and challenges. On a daily basis, people give up privacy in exchange for convenience, often with little awareness of what they are doing. A 2015 survey found that Americans place a high value on privacy. In fact, 74 percent of respondents felt it was very important to be "in control of who can get information about you."[13] Strong majorities also wanted to control what information is collected and to avoid having someone watch or listen to them without permission.[14]

Modern society is looking for ways to make the best use of big data while protecting individual privacy rights. How society decides to balance data and privacy will affect the future of everyone who uses computers, cell phones, and similar devices.

PUBLIC PERCEPTION

Opinions vary when it comes to the proper balance between privacy and security. Forty percent of adults surveyed by the Pew Research Center in 2014 said they disapproved of the government collection of Internet and telephone data as part of antiterrorism efforts.[15] Another 32 percent said they approved, while 26 percent said they were not sure.[16] Adults age 50 and older were more likely to approve of the programs, while those under age 50 were more likely to be uncertain.[17] In general, those who had heard a lot about government monitoring were less likely to approve.[18]

CHAPTER 2

DATA GROWTH THROUGH HISTORY

People have collected and stored information for thousands of years. Records were initially kept on stone, clay tablets, or paper, and all information had to be copied by hand. The invention of the printing press in the 1400s began an information revolution. Books became cheaper and more plentiful. Scientists, philosophers, and government or religious officials could quickly share their ideas with large audiences. By 1944, a university librarian estimated American university libraries were doubling in size every 16 years.[1] The output of academic journals, newspapers, and other sources of information was also increasing rapidly.

Computers, which were developed in the 1940s but not widely available until the 1970s, provided an easier way to store these growing amounts of data. However, early computers were slow and had limited memory. Still, data was collected in massive amounts, with few rules to guide what data could and should be collected and how it should be stored and used. To many businesses, it seemed easier and safer to keep data than to discard

Johannes Gutenberg invented the printing press in the 1400s.

REACTING TO TECHNOLOGY

Privacy and technology have been in conflict throughout modern history. The first mail service in the United States was established in 1775. Mail was frequently opened in transit, until this was made illegal in 1782. In the 1800s, the rise of mass media such as newspapers led to legal protections of privacy. For example, judges have ruled in court cases that private facts should not be made public. Other court cases have ruled against the use of someone's name or likeness to sell a product without permission. In the 1900s, radio and wire communication led to laws against wiretapping and spying on private communications. Laws tend to follow behind technical innovations, reacting to problems rather than anticipating them.

it, in case the information might be wanted later.

By 1997, the term *big data* was used to describe a new phenomenon. Data is simply a set of facts and statistics, collected for reference or analysis. Big data refers to extremely large sets of data. Until recently, these datasets were too big for typical software to store, manage, and analyze. Only large organizations could afford the time and expense to sort through huge amounts of data and analyze the results. Few people or organizations had the resources to access and use it.

The Internet, which was invented in 1969, was not widely used until the 1990s. It then contributed to the continued growth of big data. A wide variety of information could now be stored and shared online, including casual e-mails, college research papers, and scans of old documents. By 1999, the world was producing information more

Early computers, such as the Electronic Numerical Integrator and Computer (ENIAC), were not capable of storing large amounts of data.

rapidly than ever before.[2] This information included paper and film, but digital was the largest and fastest growing portion. People became concerned data would overwhelm the systems designed to capture, store, and retrieve it. They wondered how useful it was to keep all that data if no one knew what was there. Furthermore, they wondered what important discoveries could be buried and never found.

After the year 2000, the amount of digital data increased dramatically, but at the same time, methods of handling it improved.[3] With better software, companies and organizations of all sizes have access to the tools used to analyze large data sets. Big data was hailed as a major innovation in computing—one that could transform nearly every aspect of life. This vast amount of data impacts many aspects of society, including business, government, and science.

DATA EVERYWHERE

Almost anything a person does online is available to be discovered. Browser and search history can be tracked. Sometimes this is done by requiring the user to log in, and sometimes it is done through a file called a cookie, which stores user information to later be used by a website. Companies can also track what people "like" on social networks such as Facebook, along with the songs and videos people have streamed. Mapping software in a cell phone or portable computer tracks the user's location. Vendors can track credit card, debit, or PayPal transactions for purchases made both online and in person. Software tools can even scan the contents of blog posts, online reviews, or social media updates.

Using this kind of data, marketing companies make intelligent guesses about a buyer, predicting a variety of pieces of information, such as their gender, income, or health status. Companies can then target ads to a specific consumer, which benefits businesses. This data is

> " Nothing you say in any form mediated through digital technology—absolutely nothing at all—is guaranteed to stay private. " [4]
>
> —Farhad Manjoo, technology columnist for the *New York Times*

so valuable that an industry of information peddlers called data brokers has sprung up to buy and sell customer lists and other data to marketers. Data brokers are large companies that collect data on millions of consumers. They may then sell the data to other companies or use it for marketing campaigns. One large data broker, Acxiom, claims to have profiles on nearly every consumer in the United States. There are several thousand data broker companies throughout the world.

Having one's life recorded and scrutinized is not necessarily bad for the consumer. Companies use their understanding of customers to provide a better user experience. For example, Netflix users benefit from the company's ability to predict which movies and TV shows individuals will like. Grocery stores may give special coupons based on a shopper's buying history, saving those customers money. And often, ads that are targeted to a consumer's taste may be of more interest than ads placed at random.

ACCOUNTABILITY

In March 2015, several US senators drafted a bill called the Data Broker Accountability and Transparency Act. This act attempts to provide guidelines for regulating the data broker industry. Among other guidelines, the act would require data brokers to allow individuals to review and check the accuracy of their personal information. It would also require data brokers to allow people to express a preference to keep their information from being used, shared, or sold. This act was assigned to a congressional committee in 2015.

However, some people are uncomfortable with the idea that strangers know so much about them. For this reason, some companies may be slow to adopt certain practices out of concern consumers will complain. Other companies may also be waiting for even more refined methods of data analysis, which may be more successful. Whereas consumers may be concerned about privacy, companies may be more concerned about their reputation or the practice's success rate. As technological advances provide even more effective methods of tracking and analyzing data, companies may be tempted to reduce customer privacy in favor of business benefits.

At the core of the issue is the question of who owns this data. Is it the individual the data relates to, the device that collects it, or the company or organization handling the data collection? At this point, the matter is unsettled, so whoever has access to the data tends to use it as he or she sees fit. Some experts believe this will lead to consumer revolt and then government regulation. The next few years may determine how society balances big data and privacy.

Netflix has figured out how user ratings can predict other content those customers will enjoy.

CHAPTER 3

WATCHING CUSTOMERS SHOP

On a typical day, the average American might search for information on Google, shop on Amazon.com, and share news on Facebook. The success of those companies comes from their ability to offer users fast, easy access to information, products, and social connections. But individuals' needs and tastes differ. So, big companies use information about each customer to return the best results. Companies combine a user's account information with patterns in his or her online history. Basic information—a person's age, gender, and so forth—linked with specific behavior helps predict the customer's needs and desires. For instance, the company might guess one person will be interested in a new video game, while another would prefer to see clothing ads.

Companies like big data because it helps them understand their customers. Studies of customer behavior can help improve store layouts and what products are offered in what locations. Tracking which coupons are redeemed allows stores to offer more desirable coupons. Many customers want online stores to keep

Amazon.com uses purchase records to determine which items a customer might be interested in seeing.

track of their prior purchases, their wish lists, and perhaps even their search histories so they can be notified when an item of interest goes on sale. Online algorithms can help shoppers find what they need. Some features, such as Amazon's Customers Who Bought This Item Also Bought, may introduce users to new items of interest.

Even incorrect data can be useful. For example, people typing a search into Google may get a response that starts with "Did you mean" and provides a different spelling for one of the search words. Google remembers errors people have made in the past and assumes other people may make the same errors. Thus, by tracking not only what people search for, but also the errors they make, Google can provide more accurate results in the future.

The use of big data can have financial and security benefits for consumers as well. Search engines and some websites also allow online shoppers to compare the prices of many retailers. This can help consumers find the best price and can encourage companies to compete by keeping their prices reasonable. Also, tracking payment patterns can help merchants and credit card companies identify fraud earlier, saving consumers the hassle of discovering fraudulent charges after the fact. Data analysis thus provides benefits for both businesses and consumers.

Google uses tools such as predictive typing to help users find the information they're looking for.

BEHAVIORAL TARGETING

Targeting a consumer's individual tastes can make a huge difference in that customer's behavior. For example, some retailers use customer data from loyalty programs to create customized coupons. Companies that do this claim redemption rates on highly targeted coupons can be up to 25 percent, versus only one percent for nonpersonalized coupons.[1]

DATA FUSION

In some cases, companies and organizations may share data for mutual benefit. Data fusion merges information from several surveys into a single database. New results can then be drawn from information in several surveys. Nielsen, a market research company, provided a simple example in a report on data fusion. One survey might find people who eat canned fruit tend to be older. Another survey might find older people tend to watch more TV. Data fusion combines common characteristics to conclude people who eat canned fruit tend to watch a lot of TV. Therefore, it might make sense to advertise canned fruit on TV.

Market research companies and businesses like data fusion because it is a relatively cheap and efficient way to use data that already exists. But the President's Council of Advisors on Science and Technology issued a warning about data fusion. Because people may not be aware their data from different sources is being combined, they may not realize their privacy is compromised. Data from multiple sources may be combined to provide much more detailed data that interferes with privacy rights. Users may be

Companies can use data fusion to help decide which TV programs would be the best fit to advertise their products.

able to adjust their privacy options or opt out of tracking in some cases but not others. In other cases, they may not even realize they are being tracked. One of the big challenges of our modern age is balancing the privacy of individuals with the benefits big data can provide.

WHAT THEY KNOW

Few people would deny big data has provided big benefits for consumers. However, many people are uncomfortable with the idea of big companies knowing so much about them. Furthermore, companies can push the boundaries of privacy. For example, Target and other retail companies track buying data for each customer. The customer's ID number is tied to the credit cards used for purchases. Target also records information from coupons used, websites visited, e-mails opened, and more. Target may even buy data about customers from other companies.

Statistics experts analyze the data and identify shopping patterns. Target can then send the customer appropriate coupons. If purchases suggest a woman is pregnant, Target can provide coupons for things she might need. Target can even estimate her due date and switch to baby products such as diapers at the right time. However, some customers were disturbed Target knew about their pregnancy before it had been announced to family and friends. In fact, an article in the *New York Times Magazine* related an anecdote about an angry father who stormed into Target asking why his teenage daughter was getting coupons for baby clothes. He found out soon after that she was indeed pregnant.

We want more information than consumers are prepared to give. [6]

—Nielsen, a market research company

Target tracks information about its customers to predict which coupons each customer might use.

NOTHING NEW

Target is hardly alone in analyzing customer data. Most large retailers collect data and use analytics to determine customers' habits. Many other companies and organizations, such as banks and health insurance companies, do the same and have done so for many years.

In the 1920s, the consumer goods company Procter & Gamble conducted door-to-door market research. The information the company collected informed its decisions about product development and advertising. Today, Procter & Gamble can collect similar information more easily from social media, sales data, and other sources. Computer models can even help predict future consumer demands.

Similarly, the package delivery company UPS has been tracking the movements of its vehicles and packages since the 1980s. Now, sensors installed in delivery vehicles work with data from maps and report on pickup and drop-off times. This helps UPS plan routes to be more efficient. Not only has the practice saved UPS money, but using less fuel also means less pollution.

Other sensors used by businesses could track workers' efficiency and customer satisfaction, potentially allowing businesses to make improvements. However, some experts argue that too much focus on big data can be a waste of time and money. For example, the owner of a store might discover she could raise profits by making certain changes within the store. But that might require redesigning the store's physical layout. If the store's owner is not willing or able to make those changes, the information provided by big data did not help.

One study, reported in the *Harvard Business Review* in 2013, interviewed 51 business executives. Only a few were actually using big data to guide their decisions.[7] Those who did so saw improvements in their business performance.[8] However, in many cases, management did not properly use big data to make decisions.[9] Using big data well requires an attitude shift

rldwide Services
hronizing the world of commerce

UPS uses sensors in its delivery trucks to increase the efficiency of its routes.

throughout the company. The company must make decisions based on evidence rather than on traditions, habits, or personal tastes and opinions. People may need extensive training to learn how to do this.

Big data also cannot analyze information it does not have. For example, a convenience store could track sales to analyze how well corn chips sell. It would not be able to predict how well popcorn would sell if the store does not already carry popcorn. However, clerks working in the store might know if customers had been asking for popcorn. In this case, big data cannot replace human observations and understanding. Big data provides benefits to companies only if the company understands and uses the data properly.

CHAPTER 4

STAYING HEALTHY

Shoppers are not the only ones who have benefited from access to big data. The fields of science and health care have greatly benefited as well. An important factor is the development of the Internet of Things, a network of physical objects that can collect and share data. These objects include a wide variety of devices, including sensors that can control the lights or thermostat in a home via a phone app, city trash cans that send an alert when they are full, and many medical devices. For example, pacemakers are small devices inserted into a patient's chest or abdomen to help control abnormal heart rhythms. Recent developments allow pacemakers to send data to the patient's doctor, who can then monitor the patient remotely, saving time and money and potentially catching problems earlier.

Other devices are worn outside the body and include a variety of mobile platforms or apps that allow users to track health data. Today, many people track their physical activity using a personal device, such as a smartphone or fitness tracking watch. People can also track their meals, weight, sleep, medication, and menstrual

A woman uses a smartwatch to track the results of her workout.

cycles. In some cases, this information may be shared with research groups, enabling scientists to study more people, in more detail, more quickly. Results based on tracking sensors are more accurate than when participants self-report how long they exercised or slept.

The Internet of Things depends on connections between devices and the systems that support them. When an app tracks a user's exercise practices, this data can be saved and analyzed over time. An individual can see how his or her performance changes. This could lead to more efficient workouts and better health. Some people also feel more motivated when they track their workouts and see improvements. Friends may inspire and encourage each other when they share workout results on social media or participate in group online challenges.

Companies and organizations also benefit when users save and share health data. A company collecting exercise data from users might analyze information from thousands or millions of people. This data could be combined with information about the users' diets, sleep habits, and other aspects of daily life. Analyzing that data for large groups could lead to new insights on how human behavior affects health.

REVOLUTIONIZING MEDICINE

Scientific researchers hope access to this health data will lead to breakthroughs in the understanding and treatment of disease. With this goal in mind, the government launched the Precision Medicine Initiative (PMI) in 2015. The goal of the PMI is to develop strategies for the prevention and treatment of disease based on an

President Barack Obama promotes the Precision Medicine Initiative at an event at the White House on January 30, 2015.

individual's specific needs. The PMI intends to enroll at least one million volunteer participants. These people will provide access to their electronic health records, biologic specimens such as blood samples and DNA tests, and information on their behavior. With this detailed data, the PMI will compare participants' rates of diseases and responses to treatment. Over time, this initiative is expected to advance medicine in many areas. For example, treatments for cancer may be adjusted based on the patient's genetics. In addition, doctors may be able to better tailor the dosage of a drug to a patient's individual needs.

Research by other groups is using data from iPhones to study people with asthma, heart disease, diabetes, cancer, and Parkinson's disease. As more information is available, the apps will offer advice to the users. This means users will not only contribute to medical science, but they will also get an immediate benefit if they follow the advice.

HELP OR HARM

The Internet of Things provides many benefits for consumers. However, people often have little idea of what information is being collected and stored or how the information is being used. The Federal Trade Commission (FTC) studied 12 health and fitness apps and found the apps sent user data to a total of 76 different third parties.[1] This data included names, e-mail addresses, locations, exercise and diet habits, medical symptom searches, and more. Much of this data was sent to advertising agencies, but the FTC expressed concern that the data could be used to determine insurance rates, drug prices, or even credit ratings. Data from different apps may be combined to provide a more complete profile of someone. Privacy policies that promise information

> **"** Tonight, I'm launching a new Precision Medicine Initiative to bring us closer to curing diseases like cancer and diabetes—and to give all of us access to the personalized information we need to keep ourselves and our families healthier. **"**[2]
>
> —President Barack Obama, State of the Union Address, January 20, 2015

In 2015, insurance company John Hancock offered a free Fitbit device to people willing to use it to track their activity levels. Active people would receive perks such as lower life insurance premiums. While this program was designed to benefit healthy people, some experts expressed concern it could be used to punish the unhealthy. Jamie Court of the nonprofit group Consumer Watchdog said, "This may look like a carrot to lure new customers, but it's ultimately a stick [to punish people]."[3] He expressed fears that insurers would eventually use tools such as this to deny people coverage. Meanwhile, others claim this type of program motivates people toward healthier behavior.

will not be shared could be changed in the future. While people may benefit from tracking their own workout habits, they may not want a company collecting that information.

> The public could start seeing research as something that isn't imposed on [them], but as an activity that we all do together so that we can learn together. [4]
>
> —Ida Sim, MD, professor of medicine at the University of California, San Francisco

Many people might not consider the number of steps they walked in a day to be private information. However, security becomes more important when that kind of data is linked to personal information and medical records, as it may be with research projects that link app data to health results. Poorly secured data could be stolen and used for identity theft or insurance fraud.

Building new links between medical care, research organizations, and consumer products such as health apps could mean some health records are less private. People may worry about their ability to get proper health insurance if the insurance companies can see the health history or dietary habits they record. Health insurance companies pay out far more for some patients than for others. A healthy person may seldom use medical services, so the insurance company makes money. Someone with a chronic illness may cost the insurance company more money than the patient paid into the system. It is relatively easy to see which patients are costing the insurance company the most money. Big data can go a step further and predict which patients may cost the most in the future. Although the Affordable Care Act, a law passed in March 2010, prohibits health insurance companies from refusing coverage based on a preexisting condition, a company concerned about only its profits might look for loopholes to avoid covering these customers.

The PMI has openly stated its belief that data

SECURITY ISSUES

Laws help prevent health insurance companies from using unfair or abusive practices. Laws are of less use when it comes to illegal activity. Anthem, the second-largest health insurance company in the United States, suffered a security breach in early 2015. Thieves accessed the addresses, Social Security numbers, and employment information of 80 million customers and employees.[5] Such health information can be sold on the black market. People then use the information to defraud insurance companies with false claims or to buy drugs or medical equipment to resell. Each year, the cost of medical fraud adds up to billions of dollars.[6] People may not realize their medical records have been stolen until they hear from bill collectors demanding payment for medical procedures they never had.

should be shared responsibly. Its participants will be able to access their own health information and learn about any research that is using their data. Several government organizations, including the National Institutes of Health, the Department of Health and Human Services, and the Food and Drug Administration, are working together to ensure patients' privacy and other rights are respected. Privacy controls may vary among other research groups and businesses. The Health Insurance Portability and Accountability Act of 1996 (HIPAA) sets rules for the use and disclosure of individuals' health information for most health-care organizations. However, HIPAA privacy rules do not cover most other private businesses or public agencies. A committee from the National Academy of Sciences found that the HIPAA Privacy Rule does not protect privacy as well as it should. In addition, health-care databases are subject to security breaches. The possibilities of big data use in health care clearly illustrate the potential for huge benefits but also misuse.

RISK-BASED PRICING

Risk-based pricing is a common practice for other types of insurance. For example, car insurance companies charge more to customers who have received tickets. They might also offer discounts to customers who take a safe driving class. This practice rewards people who follow good driving practices.

> **❝** I think we need to move from what we've considered adequate security for health care into, more or less, military grade security. **❞** [7]
>
> —Victor Strecher, University of Michigan professor

FASTER FLU TRACKING

Millions of people use Google each day to search for information related to their daily activities. People turn to Google for information about nearby restaurants, traffic conditions, or even medical symptoms. Google can monitor how often certain search terms show up during a given time period or in a particular geographical region. Some researchers hope to use this data to track outbreaks of diseases.

Google Flu Trends (GFT) was supposed to be a breakthrough way to monitor the flu. By recognizing where and when the flu was hitting, resources such as flu shots could be allocated to best slow the disease's spread.

Traditionally, flu monitoring starts with reports by physicians. Launched in 2008, GFT attempted to estimate the prevalence of flu based on Internet searches for flu-related terms. GFT was faster than previous methods and initially worked very well overall. However, GFT dramatically overestimated flu levels in 2013.[8] News reports may have caused many people to search for information on the flu when they were not ill, skewing the results. After the failure, Google quietly stopped the GFT program.

Disease control experts still see a future for using big data to track and control diseases such as the flu and Ebola. Computer algorithms can be adjusted to provide better information, and they must be constantly updated. However, the failure of GFT showed the danger of putting too much faith in big data analytics.

CHAPTER 5

STAYING IN TOUCH WITH SOCIAL MEDIA

Social media users know the many advantages of such services: keeping in touch with family and friends; meeting new people; sharing thoughts, feelings, and experiences; following the news; and general entertainment. Social media sites also interact with other sites, such as online stores. Businesses use social media data, such as a user's interests and likes, for market research in order to develop better products and services. For the business, this means more sales, but consumers benefit as well by having products and services they want. Many customers follow businesses on social media in order to receive notices of sales or new products. Customers may also use social media to submit complaints or requests for assistance.

The power of social media rises when multiple sites are linked. Google+ does not have nearly as many users as Facebook, yet Google+ may know more about its users. That is because Google also owns the Google search engine, Gmail, and YouTube. Google could potentially link information from all these sites, combining

Google CEO Sundar Pichai speaks to a group of college students in New Delhi, India, in December 2015.

BULLYING GOES ONLINE

About a third of teens who have an online presence have experienced cyberbullying, often on social networking sites.[2] These platforms can allow the bully to harass a target in a public forum, leading to more embarrassment. Cyberbullies can sometimes keep their identities secret, making it harder to stop or punish them. Online harassment has led to violent attacks or even the victim's suicide.

If caught, social media users who participate in cyberbullying may potentially face legal action for their posts. Many states now have laws that address bullying, including cyberbullying. These vary by state but typically include a definition of bullying, legal processes to address it, and punishments, which can include school suspensions, expulsions, or even jail time. There are currently no federal laws directly related to bullying. However, in some cases, federal laws against discriminatory harassment may apply. These laws cover harassment when it is based on race, national origin, color, sex, age, disability, or religion.

information about what people search for on Google, what they watch on YouTube, what messages they send in Gmail, and how they interact on Google+. Google also owns DoubleClick, the largest online advertising company, and AdMob, a major mobile advertising company. Altogether, Google has a presence on more than 70 percent of websites, giving the company unparalleled knowledge of today's consumers.[1]

MANIPULATING HAPPINESS

Social media provides many advantages to users, but it also brings up privacy concerns. People are likely to share detailed personal information on social media sites, which can lead to a variety of problems. For example, posting vacation plans on Facebook lets potential burglars know the house will be empty. Many people enjoy online quizzes that may seem silly, such as what book or

Users of popular social media sites such as LinkedIn, Twitter, Facebook, and Google+ do not always know how the information they post will be used.

movie character a person most resembles. But in some cases, those quizzes can ask for detailed personal information, which is shared with advertisers, who may be the sponsors of the quiz. Since people rarely bother to check privacy policies on these quizzes, the information may be sold to other companies. Ultimately, the quiz taker does not know how that information will be used. A quiz designed to predict how long a person will live could be shared with health insurance companies. An employer might even be able to access information about an employee's personal habits.

Some results of social media usage are even subtler. In 2014, many people were shocked to discover Facebook had allowed research on its users without their knowledge. Almost 700,000 Facebook users were randomly divided into two different groups for a study.[3] For a week in January 2012, each group's newsfeed was changed. One group saw posts with more positive emotional content, while the other group saw more negative content. The study then looked at the posts made by people in each group. It found the group that saw more positive words also posted more positive words.[4] The group seeing negative words posted more negativity.[5] The differences, while extremely small, helped demonstrate the concept of emotional contagion. This concept suggests people are influenced by the words of those around them.

DIFFERENT RESEARCH RULES

Academic groups and commercial businesses conduct research. Different laws apply to each group. Academic studies typically must receive approval from an ethics review board. Commercial research does not need approval from an ethics panel. Two academic researchers associated with Cornell University were involved in the Facebook study, but an employee at Facebook gathered the data. Because the academic researchers did not have direct access to the Facebook user data, no review was required.

The ability to affect people's emotions and behavior is a powerful tool. A company such as Facebook might be able to keep users more active on its site if it provides them with a positive experience. Happy users spending more time on the site could lead to more clicks on ads, and thus more money for Facebook.

Facebook has encountered other legal challenges because of its privacy practices. In 2011, Facebook settled a suit with the FTC. The FTC had found Facebook to be in violation of the FTC Act in the United States when Facebook changed its privacy policy without warning. Some information that had previously been private, such as friends lists, was made public without advance notice. In addition, Facebook shared users' personal information with advertisers, despite claims it would not. It also allowed access to the content of deactivated or deleted accounts, despite promising these accounts would not be accessible. The FTC declared Facebook must increase its privacy and security measures. Facebook also had to accurately state what user data was private and obtain consent before making any changes to that policy. An independent audit every two years until 2031 will check Facebook's compliance.

A Facebook spokesperson said the study's goal was to improve their services and provide more relevant content to users. While this goal sounds harmless, Facebook received backlash for the way the study was conducted. Although advertisers have been trying to influence people for generations, scientific researchers typically get permission from their study subjects. Facebook users had no idea they were part of a research project.

Facebook faced legal and regulatory challenges but claimed the research was legal, because when users sign up for Facebook, they agree to allow Facebook to perform data analysis. Facebook chief operating officer Sheryl Sandberg apologized for how the study was communicated without acknowledging any wrongdoing in conducting the study. Public outrage alone might cause social media companies to avoid projects such as this one, as they do not want to lose users.

ETHICAL QUESTIONS

Many researchers and ethics experts defended the Facebook experiment. They felt the study was worthwhile because of its value to social science. In any case, social media sites such as Facebook routinely change the algorithms that determine what people see on the site. Some defenders argued it wasn't really so bad Facebook had learned how to make users happier. After all, social media sites benefit from having happy customers, so it is unlikely Facebook would manipulate people to be unhappy in the long run.

Some experts also suggested public outrage would not actually prevent such experiments but rather prevent them from being publicly reported. Psychologist Tal Yarkoni said, "By far the most likely outcome of the backlash Facebook is currently experiencing is that, in future, its leadership will be less likely to allow its data scientists to publish their findings in the scientific literature."[6] In other words, Facebook might continue to study how to affect customer behavior, but the information would only be used by Facebook itself. The information would not be used to advance science.

> **The mere fact that Facebook, Google, and Amazon run experiments intended to alter your emotional experience in a revenue-increasing way is not necessarily a bad thing if in the process of making more money off you, those companies also improve your quality of life.**[7]
>
> —Psychologist Tal Yarkoni

Facebook's chief operating officer, Sheryl Sandberg, responds to questions in an April 2014 television interview.

Other people felt the experiment showed the potential for terrible abuse. Clay Johnson, the cofounder of the technology firm Blue State Digital, said the experiment was terrifying. He asked, "Could the CIA incite revolution in Sudan by pressuring Facebook to promote discontent? Should that be legal? Could [Facebook founder and chief executive] Mark Zuckerberg swing an election by promoting Upworthy posts two weeks beforehand? Should that be legal?"[8]

Some experts called for academic ethics guidelines to be tightened and clarified to meet the new possibilities of the big data world. However, stricter guidelines on academic research would not prevent companies from using big data in market research. Nor would they prevent the kind of misuse Johnson imagines.

Zuckerberg, *left*, meets with Japanese prime minister Shinzo Abe. Johnson fears Zuckerberg could use Facebook to sway public opinion on political topics.

KEEPING THE PUBLIC SAFE

While private companies have certain restrictions on data collection, the US government has different guidelines. In some cases, the government has a greater right to information for law enforcement and national security. The government may also be able to buy data from private companies in situations where it could not legally collect the data itself. Because the government potentially has so much access to data about every citizen, some people feel the government needs stricter guidelines and more oversight.

In 2014, President Barack Obama made a speech about national security in response to the NSA information Edward Snowden had leaked. Obama began by noting government surveillance had been important throughout the history of the United States as a way to protect national security. However, he acknowledged abuse was possible. In the 1960s, the US government spied on civil rights leaders and critics of the Vietnam War (1954–1975). The 1970s brought new laws designed to prevent the misuse of surveillance against citizens. Obama

President Barack Obama spoke about NSA surveillance at the Justice Department in Washington, DC, on January 17, 2014.

noted the main security threat against the United States currently seems to be terrorist groups rather than other countries. This complicates surveillance. Spying, which was once targeted at enemy governments, now must address individuals who might be acting alone or in small groups.

The terrorist attack of September 11, 2001, led to new guidelines for government surveillance. After the attack, many citizens were more afraid of terrorists than they were of losing their privacy. However, by the time of Snowden's revelations in 2013, some of that fear had faded, and more people were concerned the government had gone too far in promoting security over privacy. In a 2014 survey, 40 percent of adults said they disapproved of the government collection of Internet and telephone data as part of antiterrorism efforts.[1] Another 32 percent said they approved, while 26 percent said they were not sure.[2]

Obama stated in his speech he felt the NSA was doing important work and following guidelines to protect US citizens' privacy. However, he noted technology was progressing so rapidly guidelines did not always keep up. He argued the United States should have a strong, ongoing discussion about the balance between security and liberty. Obama said, "The power of new technologies means that there are fewer and fewer technical constraints on what we can do. That places a special obligation on us to ask tough questions about what we should do."[3] Obama also announced specific changes to policy, as well as a comprehensive review of big data and privacy.

Terrorists attacked the World Trade Center in New York City on September 11, 2001, leading to a national climate of fear.

CRIME FIGHTERS

Data analysis can also help prevent or solve crimes at the local level. Predictive policing is the practice of using data to determine patterns in crime. Traditionally, analysts have had to review crime reports manually to make comparisons, but new technology

CYBERSECURITY ACT OF 2015

In December 2015, Congress passed the Cybersecurity Act of 2015 to expand on the Cybersecurity Information Sharing Act (CISA), which was passed earlier that year. The Cybersecurity Act of 2015 permits firms to voluntarily share cyberthreat data with the government, although companies must first remove any personal data that isn't directly related to the threat. This means the bill protects companies from liability when they share private data with the government, even if doing so violates their own privacy policies. Supporters of the bill argue this protection encourages companies to share information without fear of being sued for sharing private data. But critics of the act claim it is an infringement on the privacy of US citizens. Robyn Greene, policy counsel at New America's Open Technology Institute, stated, "The new [bill] sets up a near free-for-all for the NSA and FBI to ramp up surveillance and investigation of Americans."[4]

is changing that. Algorithms can compare data about multiple crimes, including when and where the crime happened, and details such as whether a burglar entered through the front door, back door, or window. This information might help link a new crime to a series of crimes committed by the same person or group. Knowing crime patterns can help police decide where to focus their attention. Knowing which crimes are connected can also help the police develop a better description of a suspect by comparing reports from several witnesses. Experts are currently developing and testing such approaches.

Another use of technology and big data can help identify wanted criminals. Automatic license plate readers can be mounted on police cars or on objects such as road signs and bridges. These devices use cameras to photograph license plate numbers and also record the date, time, and location of the photo. Police can identify

A police officer in Tacoma, Washington, monitors an automatic license plate reader.

cars associated with a criminal investigation. In 2011, three-quarters of local police departments surveyed were using automatic license plate readers.[5]

However, the American Civil Liberties Union (ACLU) has concerns about privacy rights with license plate readers. There is little regulation on how the information is used or how long it is stored. Private companies also use their own license plate readers to find vehicles that are due to be repossessed, and they often share the information with police. In the view of the ACLU, tracking individuals' locations invades their privacy by revealing details about, for example, what friends or doctors they visit or what events they attend. The ACLU has called for the adoption of new laws and policies regarding license plate readers. These laws would allow license plate readers to be used only by law enforcement agencies. The laws would also restrict the ability of agencies to share the data collected by the readers. In addition, the ACLU says the government should not store data about innocent people, and people should be able to find out if data about their vehicles is being stored.

PREDICTING CRIMES

Using data to solve past crimes has a clear benefit to society. However, the issue gets more complex when data is used in an attempt to predict crimes before they happen. Data can be used to identify what types of people are most likely to commit crimes and where those people live. Police trying to prevent crimes may then crack down on people and areas they expect to be a problem. This strategy can lead to a police bias against people based on age, race, gender, income, neighborhood, or other variables. Innocent people who happen to share general characteristics with area criminals could be targeted. An example of this is racial profiling, or when law enforcement targets people based on their race rather than their behavior. Racial profiling can also cause poor relationships

> In our society, it is a core principle that the government does not invade people's privacy and collect information about citizens' innocent activities just in case they do something wrong. Clear regulations must be put in place to keep the government from tracking our movements on a massive scale.[6]
>
> —American Civil Liberties Union

between police and the community, leading to people protesting or rebelling against police activity.

Some people have suggested a different option for the use of predictive policing data. Instead of cracking down on areas where crime is expected, the community could focus on prevention in those areas. Preventative tactics could include providing mentorship programs and recreational and sports activities for at-risk youth. Using big data for predictive policing could provide many benefits, but experts warn these need to be balanced with protecting individuals' rights.

DROPPING OUT?

Predictive modeling can also be used to identify college students who are at risk of dropping out of school. Ideally, and typically, this information is used to intervene early and get those students extra help. In a worst-case theoretical scenario, the information could hurt those students if teachers or the school decided to spend less time and resources on students who have a lower chance of success. As in most cases, big data analytics could be used either to benefit or to harm.

CYBERSECURITY

In the Internet age, criminals may never come into direct contact with their victims. When massive amounts of private data are stored on computers, security is an issue. While every company should have cybersecurity policies to protect employee and customer information, these policies are not always adequate, or even followed. A 2014 study found 43 percent of US companies had experienced a data breach in the previous year.[7] Yet 27 percent of companies did not have a response plan in place in case of a data breach.[9]

PREDICTING CRIME BEFORE IT HAPPENS

In 2013, the Chicago Police Department (CPD) increased its implementation of an experimental program. The CPD would use predictive analysis on the CPD's extensive crime database to predict potential crimes. The CPD's crime database already listed everyone who had been arrested. The predictive analysis algorithms identified people likely to be involved in a serious crime or violence because of their relationships to known violent criminals. This is similar to a social networking site identifying people a user may know because they are friends of his or her friends.

The CPD then began visiting people on the list of more than 400 of the highest-risk potential criminals. Some of these people did not have violent criminal records or any recent interactions with the police. The program's backers claimed it could reduce crime by warning high-risk individuals to be on good behavior. Skeptics claim the program is unfair, potentially targeting people by race or who live in a bad part of town. While the program's designers denied the algorithm used information based on neighborhood or race, it did look at factors other than criminal records. For example, people with an unstable home life, who have had problems with drugs or alcohol, or who have been victims of an assault or shooting are considered more likely to be involved in a violent crime in the future.

Despite concerns, dozens of other police departments have adapted predictive policing. While it is too early to determine the effectiveness of these programs, early results suggest a 5 to 10 percent improvement in forecasting crimes compared to traditional methods.[8]

In 2014 alone, hundreds of thousands of debit and credit card numbers were stolen and sold illegally.[10] Potentially millions of other card numbers were compromised.[11] In some cases, other personal information, such as Social Security numbers, addresses, and dates of birth, were exposed. The businesses involved included retail stores, supermarkets, restaurants, hotels, casinos, banks, nonprofit organizations, and government agencies. Some of the problems came from card processing systems infected by malware. Others were due to hacking, lost or stolen equipment, theft by employees of the companies, or accidental errors.

On November 3, 2014, a team from Norse Corporation, a company specializing in online security, visited Sony Corporation, a company known for its electronics and entertainment products, including movies. Norse was there to discuss ways of defending Sony against hackers. The Norse security team checked in at the front gate and went to the security information office. They found no guard or receptionist, and they did not even see any employees. However, computers were turned on and logged in. Mickey Shapiro, an attorney present for the meeting, said, "If we were bad guys, we could have done something horrible."[12]

Sony did not make any immediate major changes to its security. Three weeks later, on November 24, employees logging onto the Sony network found threats scrolling on the screens, the image of a fiery skeleton, and the sound of gunfire coming through their computers' speakers. Hackers had launched a cyberattack. The hackers' malware had spread through the network to machines throughout the studio lot and even across

In January 2014, police in McAllen, Texas, confiscated dozens of fraudulent credit cards related to a security breach at Target.

continents. The malware erased approximately half of the data stored on the company's computers and servers.[13] The computer shutdown interfered with many company processes, including sending messages and issuing paychecks. These events unfolded in approximately one hour. Yet the hackers had been in the system for months without anyone noticing.

The worst was yet to come. The hackers released detailed information on employees, including their salaries, performance reviews, and medical conditions. The hackers also released more than 47,000 Social Security numbers, which criminals can use to steal someone's identity.[14]

Some of the information released was simply embarrassing, such as private e-mails between executives. One producer called actress Angelina Jolie a "minimally talented spoiled brat" and an executive made racist jokes about President Obama.[15] Because of the leak, actress Jennifer Lawrence discovered she made much less than her male costars for the movie *American Hustle*. Though she largely blamed herself for not negotiating harder, she also pointed out the sexism in Hollywood and at Sony specifically.

In addition, the hackers leaked copies of several Sony films that had not yet been released. If people could watch the movies online before they were released, fewer people would pay to see the films in theaters, reducing Sony's income.

Sony executives claim they could not have done anything to prevent the attack. Some experts agree. Joseph Demarest, who was assistant director of the FBI's cyber division, said during a US Senate hearing that the malware used in the attack would likely have gotten past 90 percent of the cybersecurity options available in private industry.[16]

The Sony hack revealed details about the wages actors received for certain roles, such as Lawrence's Golden Globe–winning performance in *American Hustle*.

Other experts say Sony could have done more but its cybersecurity precautions were probably no worse than most companies. Other major companies, including Home Depot and Target, have suffered from massive hacking attacks. Ultimately, it may be impossible to prevent hackers from accessing a company's data. Yet a security breach may be less harmful if it is identified quickly. "If a [top-level hacker] wants to get in, he'll get in," Vitor De Souza, spokesman for the cybersecurity company FireEye, said after the Sony attack. "The question is, how fast do you respond? Instead of, say, taking ten terabytes of data, they might have gotten one."[17] While the Sony hack exposed cybersecurity issues, it also demonstrated how easy it is for private information to become public.

THE INTERVIEW

At first, many people blamed North Korea for the Sony hack. The North Korean government has been blamed for many cyberattacks, mainly against South Korea. Prior to the Sony hack, a North Korean government spokesperson threatened Sony if it released the film *The Interview*. This comedy shows two bumbling Americans trying to assassinate North Korean leader Kim Jong Un. The North Korean spokesperson warned if the movie was released, it would be considered an act of war and the country would retaliate. In the months after the attack, experts studying the hack said North Korea was probably not to blame after all. They suggested the culprits were more likely disgruntled Sony employees.

Fury, a film starring Brad Pitt, *left*, and Logan Lerman, was leaked online as a result of the Sony hack and downloaded nearly one million times.

CHAPTER 7

FOR THE PUBLIC GOOD?

The use of big data has changed many practices throughout society. For example, urban planners analyze location data to decide where to build roads and mass transit stops. This can help speed the flow of traffic, saving commuters time and reducing pollution from vehicles. Meanwhile, drivers can get real-time traffic updates on accidents and congestion to plan the best travel route. Some vehicles include communication modules that help drivers plan trips and improve fuel efficiency.

Big data can even contribute to promoting human rights. Using data analysis on classified ads, financial transactions, and online news sources around the world can help identify human rights abuses. This practice has helped identify patterns that indicate organized child sex trafficking is taking place.

On the other hand, some technology experts express concern too much reliance on big data analysis could have negative effects on society. Predictive analysis suggests a person's past defines his or her future. Assuming trends will always continue could help the rich and well-educated stay on their path, while making

Urban planners use big data to plan efficient mass transit routes.

it harder for poor and disadvantaged people to change their circumstances. Big data also tends to benefit large organizations, businesses, and the government, sometimes at the expense of individuals. For these reasons, consumer groups and government agencies are studying the challenges associated with big data and suggesting solutions.

PROGRESS REPORT

In February 2015, the White House released a progress report on the challenges of big data. John Podesta, a law professor and then counselor to the president, noted several areas where the government intended to make changes to current policies. These were largely in response to new possibilities to use big data technology in ways that discriminate against individuals in areas such as housing or employment.

One area of concern was student data. Data tools make it easier for students, teachers, and parents to track students' progress. Recent technology, such as apps and smart textbooks, helps students access the most relevant, up-to-date information. In some cases, technology can even adapt to an individual student's learning style. At the same time, commercial companies may see student records as a gold mine of marketing opportunities. One of the government's main recommendations was to require any student data collected in schools be used only for educational purposes. Podesta predicted Congress would show strong support for protecting student privacy.

Tools such as educational apps and smart textbooks can collect data about the students who use them.

Different people have different learning styles. For example, one person may learn better from words, by either hearing or reading information; another may learn better by using sound and music. Some people work better in groups, while others prefer to work alone.

Data analysis can help identify an individual's best learning styles. For instance, a student's choice of video games, and how well he or she plays, can help identify his or her best learning style. Data analysis can then help personalize education for that person. Ideally, this system would recognize each student's potential and help everyone achieve his or her best. However, as with most uses of big data, there is potential for abuse. For example, most people would not consider it fair if a young person's video game choices were used to help determine his or her college admissions. Yet in theory, it is possible that students could be directed into different educational and career tracks early, limiting their options.

Another recommendation in the White House report had to do with discrimination in pricing. The White House Council of Economic Advisers discovered some companies offer different prices to different consumers. Personalized pricing can be beneficial for both businesses and consumers. However, the practice can also lead to discrimination, frauds, or scams. For example, offering a variety of prices can make it easy to bait and switch customers by making false promises or hiding important details in complex contracts.

> ❝Technology alone cannot protect privacy, and policy intended to protect privacy needs to reflect what is (and is not) technologically feasible.❞ [1]
>
> —President's Council of Advisors on Science and Technology

At worst, detailed consumer information could be used to discriminate against people based on factors such as race, ethnicity, gender, or religion. On the other hand, the government report suggests big data could actually reduce such discrimination. When companies do not have a lot of information, they might make decisions based on general demographics. If people of a certain race had a higher rate of defaulting on their loans, a loan company might avoid lending money to anyone of that race. Big data gives the company far more information about each individual, so the company has more variables to choose from. The loan company might be able to tell a specific individual was a good credit risk because of his or her credit and employment history, regardless of race.

RISKS AND REWARDS

Many credit bureaus are using big data to gauge the risk a potential customer will default on a loan. Some firms study applicants' contacts on the professional networking site LinkedIn as a way to guess an applicant's character and ability to repay loans. Others look at Facebook data; an individual whose friends have well-paying jobs is more likely to be accepted for a loan. But an applicant might be rejected if one of his or her online friends has defaulted on a loan. Through data analysis, many seemingly unrelated factors can be connected to predict whether someone is a good credit risk. For example, data analysts have found applicants who type using only lowercase letters or only uppercase letters are less likely to repay loans.

DIFFERENTIAL PRICING

Differential pricing is the business practice of charging different prices for the same product. Economists also call this price discrimination. In many cases, the practice is accepted. For example, a movie theater may have different ticket prices for children, adults, and seniors or a different price for matinees versus evening shows. It is also common for airline ticket prices to increase as the date of travel nears. And car dealers may be willing to negotiate down from their list price.

Pricing is often based on demand for the product. Customers most concerned about price can take less popular options, such as the matinee at the theater. Meanwhile, people more concerned about convenience may take the more expensive option. Using differential pricing, companies sell more product overall, maximizing profits. Big data can help companies discover what prices are most successful in each circumstance.

Life insurance is another industry making use of big data to change the way it does business. Life insurance policies provide a payment to surviving family members when the insured person dies. Traditionally, life insurance companies use blood and urine tests to gauge people's health and determine insurance eligibility and rates. Big data provides a cheaper and easier way to judge an individual's health. Data brokers have extensive information on consumers, including the products they purchase, their magazine subscriptions, and their hobbies. Predictive analysis can use this data to judge a person's health based on factors such as diet and exercise habits. This could save money for both the company and the person applying for insurance, and it allows some applicants to skip supplying blood and urine samples. But the practice could

Some loan companies consider an applicant's social media presence when determining eligibility for a loan.

be used to unfairly deny some healthy people insurance based on their buying habits if companies were to depend too much on consumer data.

Many people, especially young people, are not concerned about linking their personal lives and their business or financial records. Applicants may give permission for a company to temporarily access their social media account, or a company might search the web for publicly available information on an applicant. Still, some practices could conflict with privacy laws or cause a public outcry if banks or credit card companies make too many decisions based on social media results. For example, US federal fair lending laws require American banks and lenders to follow regulations regarding what kind of information they use in order to make lending decisions. Lenders are not allowed to discriminate based on race, sex, religion, marital status, age, or physical disabilities. Many of these factors might show up on a

FAIR CREDIT REPORTING ACT

Consumer reporting agencies collect information about people to assess their credit and employment risks. At one time, the data collected included information related to a person's perceived morality, so factors such as alcohol consumption or sexual orientation might be used to deny someone a job or lodging. The Fair Credit Reporting Act (FCRA), first passed in 1970, defines how consumer credit information can be used, and morality is no longer a factor. The act also requires data be verifiable and allows consumers to access and correct their data. The law prevented some abuses, but it does not solve every problem. One study found 13 percent of credit reports had errors serious enough to affect the consumers' credit scores.[3] Still, laws such as the FCRA give consumers recourse if their information is incorrect, misused, or used to discriminate.

social media profile, and it would be hard to prove whether or not lenders accessing social media profiles considered them.

A government report on big data and differential pricing suggests current laws could address most concerns. Laws such as the Civil Rights Act of 1964 and the Fair Credit Reporting Act (FCRA) are designed to prevent discrimination. They apply whether or not the discrimination comes from big data or another source. Furthermore, big data could help identify discrimination by identifying trends. If an analysis showed higher prices were correlated with race or gender, such evidence could be used to stop that practice, either through legal action or public pressure. However, several government reports on big data recommended more study in order to prevent misuse.

CHAPTER 8

PERSONAL PROTECTIONS

In 2014, self-proclaimed "data junkie" Chris Whong used the Freedom of Information Act to request data on trips made by New York City taxis. The data included more than 173 million trips, including the pickup and drop-off locations and times.[1] The taxi numbers and the driver's license numbers had been anonymized. However, it took hackers less than two hours to decode the information and reidentify the drivers.[2] In this case, the hackers were merely trying to make a point, which they did: the technology designed to protect privacy does not always work as well as it should.

A survey of 498 adults conducted by Pew Research in 2014 found Americans place a high value on privacy.[3] Most people want to know who collects information on them and how it is done.[4] In fact, 74 percent of respondents felt it was very important to be "in control of who can get information about you."[5] Strong majorities also wanted to control what information is collected and to avoid having someone watch or listen to them without permission.[6]

In 2014, hackers used trip data from New York City taxis to prove a point about data privacy.

These preferences are maintained across different ages and genders.[7]

The degree to which most people care about privacy depends on the type of information involved. People tend to be most concerned with keeping their Social Security numbers private.[8] Their shopping habits are less of a concern.[9] Most people also want to be able to share confidential information with people they trust.[10] For example, they may want to share photographs, messages, and personal information with family or friends over the Internet.

While most people would like to control who gets information about them, few believe they have that control. Only 9 percent of survey respondents felt they had a lot of control over information collected about them in daily life.[11]

SURFING SURREPTITIOUSLY

Some 55 percent of adults who participated in the 2014 Pew Research study thought they should be able to use the Internet anonymously.[12] People gave a variety of responses for why they did not want to be monitored online. Some did not want to be bombarded by ads related to their online browsing. Some were afraid of being suspected of illegal activity due to innocent research they might conduct. And many simply felt they had a basic right to privacy, and what they did online was no one else's business.

However, survey respondents who opposed online anonymity were concerned it could allow illegal or inappropriate activity.

Many people believe they should be able to keep their online activities private. Others believe online anonymity protects illegal activity.

These people expressed concerns about terrorists, child predators, human traffickers, and cyberbullies. They wanted people tracked so offenders could be identified, and they felt people who were innocent should not be concerned about hiding their identity.

The survey also indicated what people want for themselves and what they want for others may vary. Most respondents did not feel it acceptable for the US government to monitor the average American citizen.[13] However, far more found it acceptable to monitor foreign citizens or individuals specifically suspected of criminal activity.[14] Many people seemed to believe some activities should be tracked but others should not.

WHAT HARM?

Many people believe big data compromises their privacy. A variety of organizations, such as banks, hospitals, and social media sites, collect data. These organizations may store their data for years and use it in ways that were not even imagined when it was first collected.

In some cases, companies are not concerned about their customers' privacy. In other cases, privacy may not be well protected. Deidentification was once believed to be an adequate method to protect individual privacy. Businesses could remove identifying information from a piece of data so it was not connected with a specific individual. Then the business could still use large datasets for advertising or research. However, the science of reidentification has kept up or surpassed that of deidentification. Anonymous data can quite often be linked with specific individuals again. Even if no name is attached, the relationship between the various data points can often reveal the person's identity, as demonstrated by researchers at the University of Texas. They took Netflix movie recommendations that had the user's identity removed and combined this database with resources that were publicly available online. The researchers were able to identify the individuals who had received the recommendations.

However, the reidentification process is often difficult and not cost-effective. Some experts suggest deidentification is still beneficial, so long as companies commit to protecting the data and not reidentifying the individuals involved or allowing others to do so.

> **❝** Once any piece of data has been linked to a person's real identity, any association between this data and a virtual identity breaks anonymity of the latter. **❞** [15]
>
> —Arvind Narayanan and Vitaly Shmatikov, researchers at the University of Texas who reidentified Netflix users

In theory, data could be deleted when it is no longer necessary. However, it is often hard to judge when that time comes. Future technological advances might make it possible to draw more value from current data sets. Data sets that are worthless on their own may be of use when combined through big data analysis. Academic researchers and historians may find uses for data that is no longer useful to a business. For these reasons, data sets are often saved even when they do not seem to be of use.

In a 2014 Pew Research survey, about half of survey respondents were comfortable with credit card companies and government agencies saving information for years or "as long as they need to."[16] However, most people felt online advertisers, online video sites, search engine providers, and social media sites should not save any information or should save it for only a few weeks or months.[17] No laws currently control how long most data may be saved.

Because data can be collected from so many sources and then combined, it is impossible for individuals to know what data exists about themselves. The desire to protect personal data is often a desire to prevent harm that could come from the misuse of that data. Data analysis could come up with conclusions an individual does not want shared, or the conclusions could be wrong. For example, cameras could be used to identify people at a political gathering. An assumption might then be made that everyone at the gathering shares the political beliefs of the speakers. That assumption could then be used to discriminate against someone seeking a job, or a government could use the data as an excuse to monitor someone's activities. The individual in question might never know what was happening and therefore could not protest against it.

SECURE (AND SECRET) ONLINE

Technology offers several solutions to protect information. Encryption scrambles the contents of a message so it can be read only by someone with the encryption key. Online shopping often uses encryption to provide security for information such as the shopper's credit card number. Encryption is also used to protect data in a variety of objects, such as ATMs and the key fobs that unlock cars. While encryption is an important security method, encrypted data can be attacked, most often using brute force attacks. Encryption that uses very long keys offers more security than encryption using shorter keys, but longer keys also require more resources to perform the encryption. Flaws in the code or the system can also allow attacks on encryption to succeed.

Individuals can use encryption on their computers, which helps protect against hackers or data loss when a laptop or computer is stolen. Programs can protect everything on a hard drive, or they can encrypt certain files and folders specified by the user. Any copies made to backup drives or USB thumb drives must also be protected, and the device may still be vulnerable to malware. In addition, if the encryption password is lost, the user may never be able to access the files again.

There are also programs that allow people to surf the Internet anonymously. A virtual private network (VPN) uses encryption to keep online sessions secret. These can be used to secure communications on an untrusted public network, such as a Wi-Fi network in an airport or a café. Online proxy servers hide the user's true Internet address. Other programs turn http web addresses

ATMs are protected using encryption. However, ATMs are still vulnerable to other types of theft.

into the more secure https format. Today, many web browsers have privacy settings that can be changed to prevent the browser from saving search queries, browsing history, cookies, or passwords.

Technology can help protect an individual's information, but few people take that option. For most people, the use of solutions such as encryption may seem too complicated. No more than 10 percent of adults say they have encrypted phone calls, e-mails, or text messages, according to the 2014 Pew Research study.[18] Even though most adults thought they should be able to use the Internet anonymously, only 9 percent had used a service to browse the web anonymously.[19] People also run into trouble when they do not realize deleting a message or photo does not mean it completely disappears. For example, a photo deleted from an iPhone may still be backed up in iCloud, Apple's online data storage service.

People are more likely to take relatively easy steps to protect their privacy, such as clearing their Internet browser history. People may also refuse to provide information that is not necessary for a transaction. Some even provide false or misleading information about themselves in order to preserve their privacy.

COOKIES

A cookie is a piece of data that a website stores on a user's computer. When the user returns to the website, the site reads the cookie. This allows the site to save the user's personal preferences. Users benefit by having a faster and more personalized experience on the website. They may be able to log in without typing a username and password, or they may be able to return to items saved in a virtual shopping cart. While some cookies have clear benefits to users, others are primarily beneficial to advertisers, who may track a user's every online move and sell or share the information to other advertisers. Web browsers typically have options for disabling or deleting cookies.

Getting rid of an unwanted photo may not be as simple as deleting it from the device it was taken on.

One of the best security measures is the use of strong passwords that are hard to guess. The best passwords have a mix of lower- and uppercase letters, numbers, and special characters, such as exclamation points or asterisks. Each account should have a unique password, so if one account is compromised, the others are still secure. Some services also offer two-factor authentication. This system sends the user a temporary password or number via text whenever he or she signs into his or her account. This prevents hackers from accessing an account unless they also have access to the individual's phone.

CELEBRITIES UNDER ATTACK

Public figures do not have the same legal privacy rights as private individuals. US laws are designed to allow the news media and the public to keep an eye on government officials and major figures in business. However, in the United States, celebrities are often treated as public figures, even when the knowledge of celebrities' activities does not have a public benefit.

Because of the high appeal surrounding celebrities, they are often the targets of attempts to invade their privacy. In 2014, a hacker stole and released personal photos of numerous celebrities. The list of those affected included one man and 100 women, including many famous actresses and singers.[20] In some cases, the private photos included nude pictures of the celebrities.

According to news reports, the hacker probably took advantage of a security flaw in iCloud. A secure service typically allows a user a few tries to log in before locking out the person making the attempt. However, iCloud and Apple's "Find My iPhone" app did not do that at the time, which meant a computer program could try thousands of potential passwords until it gained access. If the celebrity used a weak password, the hack was easier. Hackers sometimes guess passwords or the answers to security questions based on the target's personal data, such as middle name, birth date, or mother's maiden name. This information tends to be easily accessible for celebrities. Celebrities who used the same password for the app and for iCloud or other accounts made it easier for the hacker to access more data.

In the past, hackers who have been found guilty of leaking celebrity data have received prison time. A man who hacked celebrity e-mail accounts in 2011 received a ten-year federal prison sentence.

CHAPTER 9

FUTURE TRENDS

In 2014, President Obama called for a study into big data, focusing on how new technologies were changing government, society, the economy, and personal privacy. The 90-day inquiry was led by government officials who were experts in science, law, commerce, energy, and economics. They took feedback from the public, advertisers, the technology industry, and civil rights groups. They also discussed the matter with academic researchers and privacy advocates. The goal was to find the best way to balance all of these interests.

The group found many benefits to big data, but they also identified challenges to privacy and the potential for discrimination. The study led to several recommendations for changes in policy, including the passage of a Consumer Privacy Bill of Rights to provide standards for how personal information can be used. The group also proposed developing additional government expertise on data analysis practices so big data analytics cannot be used to discriminate against people, as well as expanding privacy protections to include non-US citizens.

John P. Holdren, cochair of the President's Council of Advisors on Science and Technology

The government has been making progress in many of these areas. The President's Council of Advisors on Science and Technology suggested privacy protection should focus on the desired outcomes rather than on technology. This means privacy policy can avoid becoming outdated as technology changes. For example, regulating the use of anonymization could not anticipate future advances that might either improve or harm privacy. Instead, regulating the ways personal data can be collected, used, and shared should provide protection regardless of technology changes. The council also recommended more research into privacy-related technologies and their use, as well as greater education and training in privacy protection.

OPT IN OR OPT OUT

One practice that is supposed to give people privacy options is "notice and consent." This setup allows people to choose whether or not they agree to a company or website privacy

THE FUTURE OF SEARCH

Joe Wikert, director of strategy and business development at Olive Software, suggests a future for computer search engines that would scan more than websites. A search might also include everything in the user's documents, e-mail, and social media streams. It could preferentially return results from websites the user has frequently visited or from their social media channels. The user could then choose to share the results in various ways. "Yes, there are countless sharing, opt-in, privacy and copyright issues to navigate before this vision becomes a reality," Wikert acknowledges. "But imagine how powerful the results will be when these capabilities become standard features in every search engine."[1]

policy. In practice, privacy notices are often long and confusing, so few users read them carefully. Those who do read them may not understand everything. Then the user is given a choice of accepting the policy or not using the service. People who want to fully participate in the modern era of online shopping, social networking, and other conveniences have little choice but to accept a policy they may not even understand.

The President's Council of Advisors on Science and Technology suggested a compromise to notice and consent practices. In a 2014 report to the president, the council noted current practices place the burden of privacy protection on individuals. Every time they want to use a new website or app, they may have to read through complex and confusing privacy notices before choosing to agree or not use the service. Instead, the council suggested third-party intermediaries could help. For example, large app stores or consumer protection groups could allow people to set up standard privacy profiles. Then that third-party group would compare these profiles to business's privacy standards. The organization would approve apps that fit the user's privacy requirements. This

Studies have shown if people see a privacy policy, many assume their personal information is secure. In reality, privacy policies often explain how a user's data will be shared. If people do not read or understand the specifics, they may unintentionally give permission to share their personal information. In addition, people may willingly disclose information in some high-risk situations and be more cautious when there is little risk. For example, many people reveal extensive private information on social networks yet would not want another party to release the same information. When people feel more control over the publication of their information, they are less concerned about privacy, regardless of the true risks. Most people understand information they reveal online may be accessible to strangers. However, they may feel the risk of a stranger actually finding the information is low, or they may decide the benefit of sharing with their friends outweighs the risk.

practice could encourage businesses to implement more popular privacy practices.

While control sounds good in theory, some experts say individuals should not be given too much control over their privacy choices. Omer Tene and Jules Polonetsky, in a paper for the *Stanford Law Review*, suggest individual consent counteracts the public good. Users may choose to keep their data private out of fear or because they want a feeling of control, opting for the strictest privacy because they fear risks that are unlikely to materialize. They may not recognize the benefits society gains from analyzing big data, or individuals may hope they can get the benefits from other people's participation without having to participate themselves.

Tene and Polonetsky argue choosing strict privacy settings may
have a negative impact on the benefits big data can offer society.

Tene and Polonetsky suggest people should be offered the
choice to opt in or opt out for certain types of data collection, such
as direct marketing. However, in some cases they feel the societal
benefits to collecting and analyzing big data are more important
than personal privacy. As an example, they note few users opt

in to provide reports of Internet browser crashes, even though this would help improve Internet use and has little data privacy risk. Tene and Polonetsky argue the desire for privacy must be balanced with potential benefits to areas such as public health or national security.

THE ENDS, NOT THE MEANS

Another academic, Alex "Sandy" Pentland, a professor of Media Arts and Sciences at the Massachusetts Institute of Technology (MIT), has proposed a New Deal on Data. This plan attempts to lay out fair rules between consumers, companies, and government. In short, the plan would declare individuals own the data collected about them. They should be able to see what is being collected and choose to opt out or opt in.

Pentland recognizes the collection of data is valuable to the individual as well as to companies. He says, "Seeing all the patterns of your life allows you to personalize medicine, personalize insurance, personalize finances. The question is, Who's going to hold the complete picture? Some credit-rating service? I hope not. Google? No. Is it going to be the individual? I hope that's the way we end up going."[3]

> " If you ask [people] what they worry about, identity theft comes in ahead of nuclear war. They don't do much about it because they don't see that they can do much, but the New Deal [on Data] is a good, plausible thing we can do today. "[4]
>
> —Alex Pentland, a professor of Media Arts and Sciences at MIT

Pentland speaks at a leadership summit in 2011.

Companies, however, are concerned that people will default to not allowing data collection. This would interfere with the ability of companies to market to those customers. Companies that now try to gather all the data they can may have to change their policies. In the long run, this could be better for those companies as well. The more data they collect, the higher the risk security breaches will cause problems. Companies that do not protect data can lose the trust of customers, and the companies could be sued or penalized by the FTC. If customers see how they benefit from data, they will become more comfortable sharing it, Pentland says.[5]

Where big data is concerned, the potential rewards to society and the potential risks to individuals are both great. As society figures out new rules and guidelines for addressing these issues,

JOB OPPORTUNITIES

As the use of big data increases, companies need more employees with expertise in that area. A report by the McKinsey Global Institute states the United States needs 140,000 to 190,000 more workers with analytical expertise.[6] It also needs 1.5 million more managers who are data literate.[7] Cybersecurity also offers job opportunities, with demand for workers outpacing other IT jobs. Some colleges offer degrees in cybersecurity. However, Ira Winkler, president and cofounder of security company Secure Mentem, points out that understanding computer systems is important in knowing how to protect them. He suggests that people interested in cybersecurity careers start by getting a college degree and then work in the computer profession before moving into cybersecurity.[8]

When companies fail to protect consumer data, such as credit card numbers, they risk losing the trust of their customers.

the ideal model would help determine the benefits of data for businesses and researchers and balance that against individual privacy rights.

ESSENTIAL FACTS

MAJOR EVENTS

» On July 10, 2008, the US government's powers of surveillance under the Foreign Intelligence Surveillance Act (FISA) expanded under the FISA Amendments Act.

» In June 2013, Edward Snowden, a former CIA systems analyst, released secret government papers that showed the US National Security Agency's (NSA) extensive spying on US citizens. Snowden went into exile to avoid arrest, while his actions set off a vigorous debate about the balance between security and privacy.

» On January 17, 2014, President Obama made a speech about national security, calling the NSA's work important but acknowledging abuse is possible. The president announced specific changes to policy and a comprehensive review of big data and privacy.

» On November 24, 2014, hackers attacked Sony Pictures, destroying much of the company's data. They released employee e-mails and personal information, and they sent five Sony films to piracy websites for free viewing.

» In February 2015, the White House released a progress report on the challenges of big data, noting several areas where the government intended to make changes to current policies.

KEY PLAYERS

>> Edward Snowden revealed in 2013 that the NSA had been spying on US citizens.

>> In 2014, President Barack Obama called for a strong, ongoing discussion about the balance between security and liberty and announced a comprehensive review of big data and privacy with specific changes to policy.

>> Alex "Sandy" Pentland, a professor of Media Arts and Sciences at the Massachusetts Institute of Technology (MIT), led the call for a New Deal on Data, a plan that attempted to lay out fair rules between consumers, companies, and the government.

IMPACT ON SOCIETY

Advances in collecting, storing, and analyzing data mean companies and organizations are collecting enormous amounts of data on most citizens. In many aspects of life, including shopping, health care, and social interactions, big data provides benefits, but these often come at the expense of a loss of privacy. How society decides to balance data and privacy will affect the future of everyone who uses computers, cell phones, and similar devices.

QUOTE

"The power of new technologies means that there are fewer and fewer technical constraints on what we can do. That places a special obligation on us to ask tough questions about what we should do."

—*President Barack Obama, in a January 17, 2014, address*

GLOSSARY

ALGORITHM

A set of steps that can be coded into a computer program to complete a process.

ANALYTICS

Logical analysis of a data set.

BRUTE FORCE ATTACK

A trial-and-error method of cyberattack where software automatically tries many combinations of possible passwords or encryption keys.

CONSUMER

A person who purchases goods or services.

CREDIT SCORE

A number assigned to an individual that predicts his or her ability to repay a loan.

CYBERBULLYING

The use of the Internet to bully or harass, including sending intimidating messages, posting unwanted photos and videos, or creating false profiles.

CYBERSECURITY

The measures taken to protect a computer or computer system against unauthorized access or attack.

DATA

Facts and statistics collected for reference or analysis.

DEMOGRAPHICS

Statistical data relating to the population as a whole, or to particular groups within it, showing factors such as average age, income, or education.

EMBASSY

The official place in a foreign country where an ambassador works to represent his or her country.

ENCRYPTION

The act or process of changing computer data into a secret code so it can be transmitted securely.

EXABYTE

A very large unit of computer data storage equal to approximately one quintillion bytes.

HACKING

The use of a computer to gain unauthorized access to another computer in order to view, copy, or destroy data.

MALWARE

Computer software meant to damage or disable computers or computer systems.

PRIVACY

Free from public attention.

ADDITIONAL RESOURCES

SELECTED BIBLIOGRAPHY

"Big Data and the Future of Privacy." *EPIC*. Electronic Privacy Information Center, n.d. Web. 10 Oct. 2015.

Harvard Business Review Staff. "With Big Data Comes Big Responsibility." *Harvard Business Review*. Harvard Business Publishing, Nov. 2014. Web. 10 Oct. 2015.

Podesta, John. "Big Data and Privacy: 1 Year Out." *The White House*. US Government, 5 Feb. 2015. Web. 1 Dec. 2015.

President's Council of Advisors on Science and Technology. "Report to the President: Big Data and Privacy: A Technological Perspective." *Executive Office of the President of the United States*. US Government, May 2014. Web. 1 Dec 2015.

Press, Gil. "A Very Short History of Big Data." *Forbes*. Forbes, 9 May 2013. Web. 10 Oct. 2015.

Tene, Omer, and Jules Polonetsky. "Big Data for All: Privacy and User Control in the Age of Analytics." *Northwestern Journal of Technology and Intellectual Property* 11.5.1 (2013): 240–273. PDF.

"You Are Being Tracked." *ACLU*. American Civil Liberties Union, Web. 15 Oct 2015.

FURTHER READINGS

Angwin, Julia. *Dragnet Nation: A Quest for Privacy, Security, and Freedom in a World of Relentless Surveillance*. New York: Times, 2014. Print.

Higgins, Melissa, and Michael Regan. *Cybersecurity*. Minneapolis: Abdo, 2016. Print.

Schneier, Bruce. *Data and Goliath: The Hidden Battles to Collect Your Data and Control Your World*. New York: Norton, 2015. Print.

WEBSITES

To learn more about Essential Library of the Information Age, visit **booklinks.abdopublishing.com**. These links are routinely monitored and updated to provide the most current information available.

FOR MORE INFORMATION

For more information on this subject, contact or visit the following organizations:

Center for Democracy and Technology

1634 I Street Northwest #1100
Washington, DC 20006
1-202-637-9800
https://cdt.org/

The Center for Democracy and Technology is a nonprofit organization working to maintain an Internet controlled by users.

Electronic Privacy Information Center

1718 Connecticut Avenue, Northwest
Suite 200
Washington, DC 20009
1-202-483-1140
https://www.epic.org/

The Electronic Privacy Information Center is an independent nonprofit research center working to protect privacy and freedom of expression.

SOURCE NOTES

CHAPTER 1. SPIES ON THE INTERNET

1. "Edward Snowden: Leaks That Exposed US Spy Programme." *BBC News.* BBC News, 17 Jan. 2014. Web. 5 Nov. 2015.

2. Ibid.

3. Glenn Greenwald and Ewen MacAskill. "Boundless Informant: The NSA's Secret Tool to Track Global Surveillance Data. *Guardian*. Guardian, 11 June 2013. Web. 14 Dec. 2015.

4. John Cassidy. "Why Edward Snowden Is a Hero." *New Yorker*. New Yorker, 10 June 2013. Web. 5 Nov. 2015.

5. Ibid.

6. "Edward Snowden: Leaks That Exposed US Spy Programme." *BBC News.* BBC News, 17 Jan. 2014. Web. 5 Nov. 2015.

7. John Cassidy. "Why Edward Snowden Is a Hero." *New Yorker*. New Yorker, 10 June 2013. Web. 5 Nov. 2015.

8. "Edward Snowden: Leaks That Exposed US Spy Programme." *BBC News.* BBC News, 17 Jan. 2014. Web. 5 Nov. 2015.

9. Barton Gellman. "NSA Broke Privacy Rules Thousands of Times Per Year, Audit Finds." *Washington Post.* Washington Post, 15 Aug. 2013. Web. 14 Dec. 2015.

10. John Cassidy. "Why Edward Snowden Is a Hero." *New Yorker*. New Yorker, 10 June 2013. Web. 5 Nov. 2015.

11. Dianne Feinstein. "The NSA's Watchfulness Protects America." *Wall Street Journal.* Wall Street Journal, 13 Oct. 2013. Web. 9 Sept. 2015.

12. Spencer Ackerman. "FBI Director Attacks Tech Companies for Embracing New Modes of Encryption."*Guardian*. Guardian, 16 Oct. 2014. Web. 14 Dec. 2015.

13. Mary Madden and Lee Rainie. "Americans' Views about Data Collection and Security." *Pew Research Center.* Pew Research Center, 20 May 2015. Web. 10 Oct. 2015.

14. Ibid.

15. Ibid.

16. Ibid.

17. Ibid.

18. Ibid.

CHAPTER 2. DATA GROWTH THROUGH HISTORY

1. Gil Press. "A Very Short History of Big Data." *Forbes*. Forbes, 9 May 2013. Web. 10 Oct. 2015.

2. Ibid.

3. "What Is Big Data?" *The Mass Big Data Initiative.* Massachusetts Technology Collaborative, n.d. Web. 19 Jan. 2016.

4. Farhad Manjoo. "The Lesson of the Sony Hack: We Should All Jump to the 'Erasable Internet.'" *New York Times.* New York Times, 18 Dec. 2014. Web. 14 Oct. 2015.

CHAPTER 3. WATCHING CUSTOMERS SHOP

1. "Big Data and Differential Pricing." *Executive Office of the President of the United States.* US Government, Feb. 2015. Web. 12 Oct. 2015.

2. "Big Data and the Future of Privacy." *EPIC.* Electronic Privacy Information Center, n.d. Web. 10 Oct. 2015.

3. Ann Cavoukian and Jeff Jonas. "Privacy by Design in the Age of Big Data." *Introduction to PbD.* Information and Privacy Commissioner of Ontario, n.d. Web. 9 Sep 2015.

4. Ibid.

5. "Big Data and the Future of Privacy." *EPIC*. Electronic Privacy Information Center, n.d. Web. 10 Oct. 2015.

6. "Introduction to Nielsen Data Fusion." *Nielsen*. The Nielsen Company, 2009. Web. 19 Oct.

7. Jeanne W. Ross, Cynthia M. Beath, and Anne Quaadgras. "You May Not Need Big Data After All." *Harvard Business Review*. Harvard Business Review, Dec. 2013. Web. 10 Oct. 2015.

8. Ibid.

9. Ibid.

CHAPTER 4. STAYING HEALTHY

1. Kate Kaye. "FTC: Fitness Apps Can Help You Shred Calories – and Privacy." *Advertising Age*. Advertising Age, 7 May 2014. Web. 15 Dec. 2015.

2. Francis S. Collins, M.D., Ph.D., and Harold Varmus, M.D. "A New Initiative on Precision Medicine." *New England Journal of Medicine*. New England Journal of Medicine, 26 Feb. 2015. Web. 14 Oct. 2015.

3. Christina Farr. "Weighing Privacy vs. Rewards of Letting Insurers Track Your Fitness." *All Tech Considered*. National Public Radio, 9 Apr. 2015. Web. 14 Oct. 2015.

4. Lia Steakley. "Harnessing Mobile Health Technologies to Transform Human Health." *Scope*. Stanford Medicine, 16 Mar. 2015. Web. 14 Oct. 2015.

5. Elise Hu. "Anthem Hack Renews Calls for Laws to Better Prevent Breaches." *All Tech Considered*. National Public Radio, 5 Feb. 2015. Web. 14 Oct. 2015.

6. "Rooting Out Health Care Fraud Is Central to the Well-Being of Both Our Citizens and the Overall Economy." *Health Care Fraud*. Federal Bureau of Investigation, n.d. Web. 19 Jan. 2016.

7. Anna Almendrala. "7 Ways Apple's New Software Could Change Medical Research for the Better." *HuffPost Healthy Living*. Huffington Post, 10 Mar. 2015. Web. 14 Oct. 2015.

8. Declan Butler. "When Google Got Flu Wrong." *Nature*. International Weekly Journal of Science, 13 Feb. 2013. Web. 5 Nov. 2015.

CHAPTER 5. STAYING IN TOUCH WITH SOCIAL MEDIA

1. Omer Tene and Jules Polonetsky. "Big Data for All: Privacy and User Control in the Age of Analytics." *Northwestern Journal of Technology and Intellectual Property* 11.5.1 (2013): 250. Web. 5 Nov. 2015.

2. "Facebook: Issues and Law." *Social Networks*. UNC Chapel Hill, n.d. Web. 5 Nov. 2015.

3. Ralph Schroeder. "Big Data and the Brave New World of Social Media Research." *Big Data & Society*. SAGE Journals, Dec. 2014. Web. 15 Oct. 2015.

4. Ibid.

5. Ibid.

6. Ibid.

7. Tal Yarkoni. "In Defense of Facebook." Tal Yarkoni blog. talyarkoni.org, 28 June 2014. Web. 15 Oct. 2015.

8. Robert Booth. "Facebook Reveals News Feed Experiment to Control Emotions." *Guardian*. Guardian, 29 June 2014. Web. 15 Oct. 2015.

9. "Facebook: Issues and Law." *Social Networks*. UNC Chapel Hill, n.d. Web. 5 Nov. 2015.

CHAPTER 6. KEEPING THE PUBLIC SAFE

1. Mary Madden and Lee Rainie. "Americans' Views about Data Collection and Security." *Pew Research Center*. Pew Research Center, 20 May 2015. Web. 10 Oct. 2015.

2. Ibid.

3. President Barack Obama. "Remarks by the President on Review of Signals Intelligence." *Office of the Press Secretary*. The White House, 17 Jan. 2014. Web. 10 Oct. 2015.

4. "Omnibus Funding Bill Is a Privacy and Cybersecurity Failure." *Open Technology Institute*. Open Technology Institute, 16 Dec. 2015. Web. 17 Feb. 2016.

5. President's Council of Advisors on Science and Technology. "Report to the President: Big Data and Privacy: A Technological Perspective." *Executive Office of the President of the United States*. US Government, May 2014. Web. 10 Oct. 2015.

6. "You Are Being Tracked." *ACLU*. ACLU, n.d. Web. 10 Oct. 2015.

7. Elizabeth Weise. "43% of Companies Had a Data Breach in the Past Year." *USA Today*. USA Today, 24 Sept. 2014. Web. 16 Oct. 2015.

8. John Eligon and Timothy Williams. "Police Program Aims to Pinpoint Those Most Likely to Commit Crimes." *New York Times*. New York Times, 24 Sept. 2015. Web. 6 Nov. 2015.

9. Elizabeth Weise. "43% of Companies Had a Data Breach in the Past Year." *USA Today*. USA Today, 24 Sept. 2014. Web. 16 Oct. 2015.

10. Bill Hardekopf. "The Big Data Breaches of 2014." *Forbes*. Forbes, 13 Jan. 2015. Web. 5 Nov. 2015.

11. Ibid.

12. Peter Elkind. "Inside the Hack of the Century." *Fortune*. Fortune, 1 July 2015. Web. 14 Oct. 2015.

13. Ibid.

14. Kim Zetter. "Sony Got Hacked Hard: What We Know and Don't Know So Far." *Wired*. Wired, 3 Dec. 2014. Web. 9 Sept. 2015.

15. Peter Elkind. "Inside the Hack of the Century." *Fortune*. Fortune, 1 July 2015. Web. 14 Oct. 2015.

16. Ibid.

17. Ibid.

CHAPTER 7. FOR THE PUBLIC GOOD?

1. President's Council of Advisors on Science and Technology. "Report to the President: Big Data and Privacy: A Technological Perspective." *Executive Office of the President of the United States*. US Government, May 2014. Web. 10 Oct. 2015.

2. Josephine Mason. "Ashley Madison Hacking Has Porn, Hook-Up Sites Scared." *MSNBC*. MSNBC, 24 Aug. 2015. Web. 7 Mar. 2016.

3. "Section 319 of the Fair and Accurate Credit Transactions Act of 2003." *Commissions and Staff Reports*. Federal Trade Commission, Dec. 2012. Web. 14 Oct 2015.

CHAPTER 8. PERSONAL PROTECTIONS

1. Vijay Pandurangan. "On Taxis and Rainbows." *Medium*. Medium, 21 June 2014. Web. 17 Oct. 2015.

2. Ibid.

3. Mary Madden and Lee Rainie. "Americans' Views about Data Collection and Security." *Pew Research Center*. Pew Research Center, 20 May 2015. Web. 10 Oct. 2015.

4. Ibid.

5. Ibid.

6. Ibid.

7. Ibid.

8. Ibid.

9. Ibid.

10. Ibid.

11. Ibid.

12. Ibid.

13. Ibid.

14. Ibid.

15. Omer Tene and Jules Polonetsky. "Big Data for All: Privacy and User Control in the Age of Analytics." *Northwestern Journal of Technology and Intellectual Property* 11.5.1 (2013): 251. Web. 5 Nov. 2015.

16. Mary Madden and Lee Rainie. "Americans' Views about Data Collection and Security." *Pew Research Center*. Pew Research Center, 20 May 2015. Web. 10 Oct. 2015.

17. Ibid.

18. Ibid.

19. Ibid.

20. Alan Duke. "5 Things to Know about the Celebrity Nude Photo Hacking Scandal." *CNN*. CNN, 12 Oct. 2014. Web. 8 Nov. 2015.

CHAPTER 9. FUTURE TRENDS

1. Joe Wikert. "Here's How Search Will Evolve and Become More Powerful." *Joe Wikert's Digital Content Strategies*. Joe Wikert's Digital Content Strategies, 19 Oct. 2015. Web. 21 Oct. 2015.

2. President's Council of Advisors on Science and Technology. "Report to the President: Big Data and Privacy: A Technological Perspective." *Executive Office of the President of the United States*. US Government, May 2014. Web. 10 Oct. 2015.

3. Harvard Business Review Staff. "With Big Data Comes Big Responsibility." *Harvard Business Review*. Harvard Business Publishing, Nov. 2014. Web. 10 Oct. 2015.

4. Ibid.

5. Ibid.

6. Omer Tene and Jules Polonetsky. "Big Data for All: Privacy and User Control in the Age of Analytics." *Northwestern Journal of Technology and Intellectual Property* 11.5.1 (2013): 251. Web. 5 Nov. 2015.

7. Ibid.

8. Ira Winkler. "How to Get a Job in Computer Security." *Computerworld*. Computerworld Inc., 8 Sept. 2014. Web. 17 Oct. 2015.

INDEX

ABOUT THE AUTHOR

M. M. Eboch writes about science, history, and culture for all ages. Her recent nonfiction titles include *Chaco Canyon*, *Living with Dyslexia*, and *The Green Movement*. Her novels for young people include *The Genie's Gift*, a Middle Eastern fantasy; *The Eyes of Pharaoh*, a mystery set in ancient Egypt; *The Well of Sacrifice*, a Mayan adventure; and the Haunted series, which starts with *The Ghost on the Stairs*.